Rockabye

ROCKABYE

Patricia McCarthy

First published in 2018 by
Worple Press
Achill Sound, 2b Dry Hill Road
Tonbridge
Kent TN9 1LX.
www.worplepress.co.uk

Cover image: Marc Chagall, *La maison rose*, 1966 Chagall ® /
© ADAGP, Paris and DACS, London 2018

Printed by imprintdigital
Upton Pyne, Exeter
www.imprintdigital.com

Typeset and cover design by narrator typesetters and designers
www.narrator.me.uk
info@narrator.me.uk
033 022 300 39

ISBN: 978-1-905208-39-5

Acknowledgements

Some of these poems have appeared in *The Guardian* online, *Acumen*, *The London Magazine*, *Poetry Salzburg Review*, *Temenos*, *The Irish Times*, *Envoi*, *Molossus World Poetry Folio #50* (New Delhi), *The Compass Magazine, Hearths II* (New Orleans) and the anthology *Poets Aloud Abu* (Ink Sculptures Ltd, Cork, Ireland)

'Childless Woman' was commissioned for the *Golden Spoon* Gwendolyn Brooks anthology (University of Arkansas Press, 2017), using acronyms from lines of her work.

'Dirty Old Men of Dublin' was runner up in the National Poetry Competition.

'The Royal Kumari' was shortlisted for the National Poetry Competition 2016.

Man must be pleased; but him to please
Is woman's pleasure; down the gulf
Of his condoled necessities
She casts her best, she flings herself.
How often flings for nought, and yokes
Her heart to an icicle or whim,
Whose each impatient word provokes
Another, not from her, but him;
While she, too gentle even to force
His penitence by kind replies,
Waits by, expecting his remorse,
With pardon in her pitying eyes;
And if he once, by shame oppress'd,
A comfortable word confers,
She leans and weeps against his breast,
And seems to think the sin was hers
    – Coventry Patmore: 'The Angel in the House'

Domestic violence should be punished more severely than similar attacks against strangers outside the home, according to draft guidelines published by the Sentencing Council for England and Wales. The recommendation reflects a shift in public attitudes towards domestic abuse. Forty years ago police officers often ignored complaints by wives against their husbands. The new advice to judges says an offence in a domestic context makes it more serious because: 'Domestic abuse is rarely a one-off incident; it is likely to become increasingly frequent and more serious the longer it continues, and may result in death.'
    – *The Guardian*, 30 March, 2017

'Every formal process proceeds from a private one'.
    – Stravinsky (from *The Poetics of Music*)

For battered women, whoever and wherever they are

Contents

Prologue: Writer's Block

Decade after decade the nib hung,
poised like a buzzard to attack the page,
but no word formed in longhand cursives.
Gagged, it seemed, by a tarred rope,
or caught in a stutter, without a tongue,
she was nervous of clearing the blockage.
And the nib hung in an afterlife
while the ink swilled with a slip and a slop
in its bottle: a miniature ocean swinking
with the wrecks of a time so suppressed
it might never have happened. There,
stripped of her mortal coil, of everything,
she did not need buoys and compasses,
a harbour, rowing boat, water or air—

nor for kind-hearted Memory to delete
the bad, and allow misremembering. Decade
after decade even silence was not itself
since there was no sound behind it to press
into syllables of witness. Blank notes,
in the glass bottle from Hades,
surfaced from sandbanks that shelved.
Inks splashed the waves' white crests,
scrimshawed drowned bones—their tides,
greenish-blue, blackened by nights
as mariners lost port, then starboard lights.
Her nib hung, still, when landlubbers
chorused *O hear us when we cry to thee*
For those in peril upon the sea.

1

The Shiver

Not the childhood shiver under a towel
with goose-bumped skin after a swim
in the refrigerated sea on Killiney Bay.

Nor the shiver of a rigor like that
from malaria lying dormant in your father
decades after his time in the Tropics.

This: with chattering teeth and white face
on a sultry summer night, escaping
to the kitchen from a fist in a bedroom—

and your father asking, 'What's wrong?
You can't be cold'. But you never saying
in case of repercussions as the kettle bubbled.

Its steam deleted you and your terror
so you could protect your father from
worry, and join him with a cup of strong tea.

A Sisterhood

i

Sarola. Your name a song, my beauty-queen ayah.
I remember the tinkle-tinkle of your ankle bells
when you floated through rooms and courtyards,
your long cotton kurta transformed on your body
into the sail of a sari, your sweeping-brush a sceptre.

You drilled me in Nepali, showed me how
to outstare monkeys at the window, how to wield
a stick to ward off packs of rabid dogs;
how to darn the mosquito net with a single hair.
You told me in which tree rattlesnakes coiled,

saved me from the one that had killed the mali
as it reared up at the door. Your long black plait
was a metronome by which I kept time to the beats
in your pulse and mine, my darning kit of sympathy
all I possessed—to mend the rips in your heart.

ii

Sarola. You confided in me your life story scented,
once, in jasmine, but taken over by Kali,
the dreaded goddess. You described your trek
over precipices, weeks long, on bare feet,
in flight from an abusive uncle in your Gurung tribe,
to a struggled-for dignity in the incense-filled city
of Kathmandu. How you hid behind the bougainvillea,
slept on mimosa or on the back of an ox sprawled
in the street. I heard how the men grabbed you,

how your husband kicked your pregnant belly
and you fled again: two tiny children to shelter
in a shack smaller than a stable, no light, no water
except what fell from the sky in your eyes.

iii

Sarola. My next memory. Finding you on a track,
hand at your throat: 'Bone choking' you kept
stammering. For help, you had gone to offer puja
to Durga in the temple of Shovabhagurati.

My own hand then in yours in the hospital
on the Ring Road I took you to, after a search
over potholes, fifty miles wide, for horse serum
in a land with no horses—to counteract lockjaw.
No daylight allowed in case of convulsions,
the gaps for windows stopped up with black rags.
My finger on the swab to hold it in place
after each injection, your exquisite face aged
a hundred years overnight. Then the space in the bed,
your treatment unfinished. Unseen, you
had discharged yourself as if imprisoned by force,
your chances of survival slimmer than your waist.

iv

Sarola. Weaker than weak, you swallowed
the bottle of vitamin tonic I found, slept
with your children on my spare woollen blankets
over the straw. And once again, stronger than
a mountain, you swirled through rooms, wiping

5

marble, brightening the copper. When I knew
I was leaving, I invited a local lady doctor—
your puzzled look when I had tried to explain
in English— to whisper to you behind a curtain
that what you had had was no common cold;

the main cause of death among women:
secret abortions from rusted coat hangers,
and buckled spokes of bicycle wheels, to avoid
beatings, banishment if out of wedlock.
You stepped back, bowed low your head.

V

Sarola. We hugged each other in the stairwell,
cowering from male voices edged in thunder.

I wonder now if you ever wore the long gowns
tailored for me from wild silks that I gave you

to find your prince—or sold them for an income
to keep your family; if you killed any of those snakes

and took out their eyes to stop them following you
everywhere ever after. Little do you realise

I search TV documentaries, newspaper magazines
on Nepal for you. Decades later, I hear still

the sizzle of your dahl, garlic, onion and potatoes
in the pan for your only noonday meal. I know

how to carry burdens—the way you showed me:
on my back, a band around my forehead to take

the strain, giving in to their weight by bending
gracefully in two as, uphill, you used to do.

Burdens can be kindling, you proved. Perhaps
you sense that I wish coral and orchid trees

for whatever world you find yourself in;
how, in my native landscapes, I think of you.

Rockabye grandfather

Rockabye, rockabye, rockabye rock
I see you on Facebook cradling
a grandchild that could have been mine.

Such tenderness, care as you rockabye,
rockabye, rockabye rock. Could the shadow
on your lined face—under those cheekbones

which jut out still like blades—be that
of the one, a generation before, gouged
out of me at fifteen weeks. The back street.

The woman in green, illegal overalls.
No killers for the pain that seared through
every threshold, every carved temple,

the light kept on all night if I wouldn't give in,
the door locked, my passport taken.
Forced into it in Kathmandhu—rock,

rock, rockabye, rock. Your swaying arms.
Is our deleted he or she a guilty glint
in the faded cobalt of your eye, a regret

that catches just the odd time in your breath
for what we could have shared? Rockabye.
But no. You didn't rock me nor that foetus

not quite a bulge. And well you might
rockabye, rock… mellowed perhaps now
in white-haired years. Much as I want

to forgive you, I cannot help seeing—
on the screen—a Bluebeard with all the keys
to my youth, my age, my childless future.

Overseas still, you swan on. Family fun.
I wish your grandchild well, to forget
the years I had as your virgin bride, the shock

at your night terrors, hands round my neck.
Hardly that rockabye grandpa—indulgent
as you rockabye, rockabye, rockabye rock,

lullabies in your arms, feather breath on your chest.
Up to me to rockabye, rockabye rock, long ago
on the broken bough, our baby that did fall.

The Royal Kumari

(a young girl child chosen to be a goddess in Kathmandu)

Imagine being taken from your mother under the jacaranda
which dressed you in its violet flowers, and to be chosen
for your body like a banyan tree, for your skin never pricked
by a rose thorn, not a drop of your blood yet shed.

Imagine being wanted for your neck curved as a conch shell,
for your lashes curly as a cow's, a fish-eye—*agni chakchuu*—
painted on your forehead to give you powers of perception,
the universe in your womb, your mother's lullabies far off.

Imagine the formality of your red outfit threaded with gold,
the tight topknot of your black hair a match for your black eyes,
thirty two tests of perfection to pass, alone with severed heads.
Imagine having to pick, from heaps, the clothes of the Kumari

before you, wondering if her skin was the dress left behind,
    silken
to your touch. On the night of the Kalratri, you must have
    wished
to undo your mother's dream of the crimson serpent,
    proving you
the one to be sacrificed to Kali along with water-buffaloes

and goats. Agile at skipping, running, what torture to be
    carried,
always, on a gilded palanquin, your feet forbidden the
    ground, paraded
outside only thirteen times a year. No playmates, just petitions
to respond to, devotees to counsel and bless. In your
    tiptilted country

of a thousand unscripted languages of ice, snow, perpendicular,
chasm, rock-face, summit—imagine having to learn a sign
    language
that forced you to fake tears, laughter, to rub your eyes, clap
your hands and tremble—for predictions of death, fear of a
    king,

ruin. Imagine the shame of your first woman-blood's letting,
cast as a mortal again, soiled, on soles too soft for walking back
across Durbar Square into a worse isolation than peeping
    like a doll
from a palace window. What would become of you:
    scratching yourself

into a carving on a wooden temple? Or, with a girl child,
    telling her
to hide with bats that hang upside down from eucalyptus groves,
to tear her skin with jagged leaves of the thorn-apple flower,
then dance under the jacaranda, rejected as a Kumari.

A different kind of prison

They were always there at the window
when I awoke, nostrils squashed

against the pane, gnarled fingers
tap-tap-tapping: macaques, threatening
entry. As if they were the gaolers,

myself in the cage of a foreign zoo.
'Never look a rhesus monkey in the eye',

it was said. But I caught a stare
that the Brahmin priests and sadhus
warned was a dervish's glare.

Though a mosquito net hung over me
like an outworn bridal veil, holed

by paddies, threats, rages, it offered
no protection from the wizened faces
of these temple primates that overheard

my thoughts and climbed my dreams.
Swinging from my fears, they fisted

the only nuggets of light I managed to save—
in solitary confinement even by
my husband's side. From some cave

in Pashupatinath I presumed they had come.
There, on stone linga, they masturbated

at teenage girls gliding by, wrapped
in smoke from burning pyres on ghats—
while the Bagmati's brown waters lapped

against worn feet of washer-women
wringing out kurtas and saris, bodies curved

towards the Ganges for a new incarnation.
They were always there at the window,
older than time, as if I was their creation.

Even with a flower

You must never hit a woman, even with a flower
    Old Hindu saying

Never hit a woman, even with a flower…

He struck each book that stuck out of line
on the shelf, gashing words until they leaked
    from their print. Texts scribbled upon by her
in margins he hurled from the window
    into the open mouths of passers-by.

Never hit a woman even with a flower
like an orchid whose vulva bees enter…

Her short skirts he yanked down until
they stretched longer than his mother's, silks
    swapped for frumpy tweeds and sackcloth
no man would admire. He positioned her
    like a piece of furniture, castors removed.
When visitors came, he wiped surfaces clean…

Never hit a woman even with a flower—
its petals crushed by hot, humid air…

    table tops, shelves, sills, dressers.
No pulse of life, no germ in his clinic.
    And then he posed, a stiff upper-lip charmer.
Deportment rigid. Host of hosts.
    If a speck of dust or a drip from coffee
marked the floor, he would grab her hair,

Never hit a woman even with a flower
like the satin-finish of a poppy, feather-soft…

shove her down on all fours to wipe it up.
His face unrecognisable, twisted in a rage—
    white, narrowed eyes, an ogre's thin lips.
Yet his friends called him a lamb,
    could never imagine him raising his voice.
had never heard the chairs he slammed—

No, never hit a woman with anything at all,
least of all a flower, a feather, blown thistledown…

    against walls as the fit took him. And then—
Alpha male, the doctor labelled him: in need
    of more sport—his fists, knuckles whiter
than his face, would force their way inside her,
    strike at her every thought and feeling, puncture
her lungs, disrupt the beats in her heart.

Never hit a woman even with a flower,
or breath, or puff of smoke, or whip of wind…

Tied down inside and out by him, she
    studied the bruises on her arms, blues, blacks,
yellows—like marbles played with
    by children, or pebbles picked from the beach.
The valiums sneaked in she was hooked upon
    to stop the blinding light, the smothering sky.

Never hit a woman even with a flower.

Depersonalised

In times of extreme stress we lose our boundaries
   C G Jung

Bring in the lapidaries. Let them polish
into a cabochon the stone you become
in the bleakest times. Let them pretend

its yellow-green comes from powdery beads
of lichens—that it has the dignity of a gravestone
carved with your living moments, no epitaph.

May you wear it around your neck
as you watch your self far off in the hard skins
of other people and animals, name-less,

estranged from the world you have inhabited.
Be prepared for hunters to come and steal
those skins which they will tan and cure,

then sell in markets to be worn by slaves
who, unknown to you, balance your troubles
on their heads and tiptoe over penance-dealers

of pebbles red hot from a relentless sun.
Warn the lapidaries, though, that—should
a devil re-model yours into the boulder

of Sisyphus—they will have to stop its roll
for your sake and let an angel break open
the entrance to the tomb for your resurrection.

Fairytale reversed

You don't want the fairytale reversed.
You want him to be that Prince with a gauntlet
and castle—who fits on your foot a glass slipper:
You don't want smashed windows and doors,

to hide underneath your princess dress.
You want the psychiatrist he won't see
to turn into the coachman who drives the horses
down the alleyways of his troubled psyche,

behind the twists and conflicts, to find
excuses like treasures there to explain him.
At midnight, you don't want the victim
to be yourself who tries to run on bound feet;

the coachman and horses to turn back into
mice, the coach into a pumpkin. You wonder
if he ever was that prince, the ugly sisters
and wicked stepmother manifestations

only of what can turn up in anyone's past
with their envy, control, jealousy. You want
to continue as if in that ball day and night-long,
even in rags, though you no longer believe

in happy-ever-afters. More a victim
than you, of his own terrors badly played out,
you want to rescue him from the drawbridge
that pulls up to let in enemy shadows.

They fester in locked chambers and parade
through his veins until the drawbridge
clanks down again. And the fairytale retreats
to hand-made pages, long ago and far away.

Fortune-Teller

Wisdom is a butterfly
Yeats

He seemed washed up by the monsoon in his saffron robe,
turban studded with sequins, eyes like brown crystal balls
ready to be taken out of their sockets, spun and scried into.

Bone-dry while the rain pelted down on him, he would come
no further than the porch, his stick for fighting off rabid dogs
balanced across his sandalled feet like a makeshift threshold

to a cycle of worlds he divined without acromancy, birth charts.
Holding me in the complicity of his gaze, he folded my fingers
over the lines in my palm, then delicately took my hand

as if it were a sheet of rice-paper from which he teased
my life story so accurately I felt I must have written it for him
in invisible ink. His voice rose and fell in unison with rishis

and the plainsong of nuns from my childhood. Flabbergasted
at his insights, I did not care whether he was a whirling dervish
in disguise or an incarnation of Vishnu, Ganesh, Shiva

as long as I could be the butterfly he said I was: the Brimstone,
Painted Lady, Least Grass Jewel, Purple Sapphire Circle,
Oakblue; and could migrate across hemispheres seen and
        unseen

strong in fragility, living much longer than the single day
that faraway Nature lessons had taught, beyond the division
of opposites—into a new wakefulness where all gods were one.

In a gash of sun between black clouds the next day when I
   went
to pay him in Durbar Square, he was illuminated,
   surrounded by
a protective circle of fritillaries. I aired my wings and was gone.

Repatriation

Royal Nepal airlines: her escape
on the pretext of an infection.
The terrible deed done following
his threats of ending it and her

if she kept it. The plane, a god
to the young uniformed pilot, rising
up, up inches from the mountain sides...
Namaste, Namaste... away from

the airport ground with its wrecks,
not just of fuselages but of foetuses,
bits of them, him or her,
not it, a throb still in her temple

pulled apart by rats infected
with the Plague, wrapped in incense
from joss sticks, spices... wafting
over her sense of abandonment.

Babies everywhere, in her head,
on summits, Chagall's couched
in moon crescents, flying in formation
with the plane, swaddled in saris,

balanced in the radar of vampire bats.
And then the landing. The Delhi
of her disaster, her empty womb
on the carousel: baggage unclaimed.

Refuge

In my mother's flat I squatted, terrified

of shelters where some of the women
were the abusers, fists used on their men.
In a dressing gown all day, I hunched
over the dining room table, scribbling.

She was so understanding, my mother,
simply letting me be, not ordering me
out under the tulip tree, nor downtown.
No inquiry about my notepads, but praise

for the hours I practised Mozart's sonatas,
allegros, andantes, allegrettos, adagios,
sinking my emotions into notes on the piano
tickled, once, by my childhood hands.

It had kept its tone in its upright frame
and somehow held me as I swayed to stories
I invented, not my own, while I played.
Page after page of words, unedited, transcribed

themselves into the music until language
and melody were one. And the sash windows
slid down of their own accord to let in the sun
that constructed a shelter of dappled light

sited in in my mother's cradling smile.

Dulce Domum

*(on a small plaster model of an American house
found in a junk shop)*

I could have lived in that house made of icing sugar
on top of a cake's mound, never melting in summers
prinked by cherry blossom, nor an igloo in winter.

Maryland or Virginia, I think it would have been
where I baked cookies, pumpkin pies for Thanksgiving—
for the children I nearly had, diapers flapping from a line

like flags to which I was newly sworn. My English accent
would have slid into a measured drawl, sawdust logs
have guaranteed twelve colours twirling, silent

in the grate of a first marriage not meant to go wrong.
Weather-boarded, I did appear, though, at the door
on a cobbled Georgetown street, desperate to belong.

On three storeys, I checked in and out of maple trees,
dogwood, lilac—as the foundations swivelled
from block to block, bug meshes broke and jangling keys

composed their own percussion. A waving bamboo screen
hid me from a Bluebeard, boundaries gone. Had my name
remained joint on the residence, it could have been mine

long after it blew up, gunrunners pinned to its yard walls.
In its hollow centre I would have entertained Romeos, wine
pumping my heart without air-conditioners, while the Fall

lasted forever, dying the Blue Ridge Mountains a blood red.
Once every fifth season, locusts, in a plague, dropped their skins
like leaves of a journal I should have written, never to be read.

But look, the house has shrunk, no fireflies for lanterns,
no Latin lover bowing the steps up to the front porch
with a regular, tap-dancing tread. From the balcony, to turn

my head, no drifting rhapsodies. All the blinds
are down, the house dirty-white on its mildewed cake—
not even a grain of sugar to ghost what I left behind.

Dancing around her

Rilke, Tennyson and the french lover
dance around her, hands joined, talk
to her in different languages, one voice
over the other in polyphonic strands
of understanding in this hostile land.
Here limousines squeak around corners
like gangsters' cars in films, suburban walks
tricky with no pavements, no choice
of routes downtown around numbered blocks.
Rows of offices and shops fall on top of her
unless she cowers under a golfing umbrella,
a stranger to herself since the seismic shock
of a call's headline, long-distance: her father
killed on a road. A world changed forever.

Rilke, Tennyson and the french lover
form a circle of protection around her
when high-rise blocks turn black. Surfaces
taken for granted have a surreal gleam
like strangers' faces that laugh at her
for what they think is the quaint grammar
of her broken English. Before them, she loses
her breath, words deleted in a silent scream.
She is unable, now, to cross a road unless
hanging onto an arm, anyone's arm; can't
drive a car because all cars are murderers;
can't cope with what she tries to suppress
in elevators, apartments; prays fate will grant
her father another chance, this just a scare.

Rilke wraps her in his angels' wings,
Tennyson mirrors her loss with his own.
And the french lover she didn't mean
to have looks after her at the request
of her husband who, this Christmas, is going
home on a charter flight, leaving her alone.
Over oysters cooked in their shells, she leans
on acute and grave accents, dressed
in liquid, Mediterranean eyes. Suspended
in a bubble, and a woman once more,
she is functioning, free, composing feathers
for her father's deathbed, safeguarded
from a husband who tears up the scores
of Rilke, Tennyson; tightens her tethers.

Portrait: Red Indian

I sit with him in his portrait's frame as in the sepia glow
of his tepee, listening to his silence in the wet grass,
to phantom herds of pinto ponies as headdresses rustle past.

I puff from his sacred pipe to gain good will, and learn
the voice of the love-flute, the favour for woman and man,
its laments smoking blue his veins, in celebration.

I imagine myself his squaw, clicking teeth worn down
by the leather I chew, my porcupine quills flattened
for embroidery of frontiers on pounded lands patterned

by battles and treaties. If only I were Corale-Of-Horses,
Thin-Elk. I have none of their skills as I stitch only words
onto waking dreams. I cannot handle the Thunder-bird

dreaded by his tribe which flaps against my window
at night, squawking its own name: *Beyoka, Beyoka, Beyoka.*
Yet in a guiding light, I feel a weathered hand on my shoulder.

Jekyll and Hyde

Yes, he was a Cary Grant lookalike.
On a bed of roses, said colleagues
at work. She tried to banish
his gargoyle face to the disused privy
in the back yard, to convince herself
he would rot there down to his skeleton.
But he would emerge with an aura
of sulphur fumes from old excretions,
twice as terrible… She remembers
only too well the dinners in beamed inns,
when he wore his handsome face,
the walks through green glints of parkland
that she naively believed would go on forever.
Yet, after his threats, never tongue-in-cheek,
she would stand outside in the early hours,
the dark down her throat, trembling,
a drainpipe all she had to cling to
as the rain dripped down her back, desperate
for the fire brigade, for anyone to save her.
She should have known better. Beware
the Cary Grant lookalike, the only child
spoilt, never said No to. Beware
the switch from Jekyll to Hyde.
Bed of roses, damask, double thorn.

The Lover

Of course he had to re-appear,
his long dark dreadlocks,
as he bent over her, a tent
in which she could be
reincarnated as a squaw,
an Indian princess swathed
in rippling saris, a new version
of her accustomed self,
human again and a woman
lit by the jewels in his eyes.
Tall, married and French,
he scribbled secret notes
to her on cigarette packets,
his very presence magnetic.
His touch was that of a cellist,
his charm that of a Romeo
with geraniums and candles.
As he polished her skin,
he was her animus, found
at last, the one never got over,
the illicit impossible man
with a phoenix's wide wings.
She never knew if he was real
or conjured from air by her need
for reassurance. Vulnerability
was no excuse. Yet under
the tabernacle of his dreadlocks
it felt like worship,
idolatrous, insane. Guilt
tapped on her eardrum,
calling her—despite the grace—
a trollop, a tart, a whore.

Prayer to Bacchus

Bacchus, god of wine, spare me your orgies.
But when yer man hits the smashed bottle
of his temperament, deafen me to the alcohol,

one hundred percent proof, in his words
that hurtle at me like popped corks. Take me in
to a well-named vineyard, dignity my sobriety.

Let me dance without fear on tabletops—
animating what his slurs kill off.
Uplift me with a good cuvée from your cellar:

velvet swigs for my mouth that requires
to pronounce verses as saviours from
his blackest forked tongue. Protect me

from broken glass. I want to be more
than the crossbones and skull on his labels,
appellation controlée. As I tread your grapes

give me their skins to wrap around mine,
youth-taut, and a nose for who I am,
and still could be, in the ghost company

of my lived-in and unlived selves. Taste
the vintages of my best years, and in return
offer me a robust red, full bodied, whites

dry, mellow, fruity. During fermentation,
compose coping strategies for me, educating
my palate with sips of understanding matured

in oak. Lay me down as if chosen, far
from this Gethsemane where water changes only
into its own stagnancy. Re-, O re-invent me.

His Say

He had his say all right: at the time.
She might as well have been swapped
for goats, lost at dice, lengths
of her hair sold by the yard by a sahib

who chewed betel nuts while slipping
opium beneath the innocent lids
of the children they didn't have
to keep them quiet on prayer mats.

He had his say all right: marching her
down to some office to sign her name
off the house, the man behind the counter
astounded as she took up the pen.

In his suave cashmere suit, shoes
of lizard-skin, and outside the law,
he threatened to leave her sleeping rough
on a park bench; said he was suicidal

unless she'd stay when he'd give her
as many children as the old woman
who lived in the shoe. But this was
no nursery rhyme—in her purse

less than he'd have paid a call-girl.

D I Y Divorce

i

All morning she practised unmaking the bed—
a bad domestic, dismantling frames
which filled while being emptied with scenes
touched up by memory's lying light,
urging the abandonment of any legal fight.

Other pictures, vindicating her action, escaped
from black polythene bags to scar her
invisibly. The worst traumas vanished—
not biodegradable but as if they had never been
into a light tinged with a pantomime green.

By afternoon, the rain had formed ropes
on which old ringers swung from belfries
long defunct. White ribbons of spray
trailed—in sudden shreds—from limousines,
dummy brides in windows were in smithereens.

ii

Storm clouds gathered in consenting parties
over the multi-storey grounds for divorce,
littered with broken vows. A petitioner
in this case—neither woman nor wife—
she pretended not to have had a former life

and to enjoy waiting forever in limbo—
unborn, unchristened—to inherit a stigma
from society. As if casually shopping in a world
of couples, she walked past her own levels
of tolerance in the wet where hissing devils

tightened their grip on her neck, warning
that a future 'freedom' with no job or home
was as absurd a proposition as a heaven.
From DIY shops, well-stocked
with what united, bound and interlocked—

short on what prised apart, she took
paint-strippers, pliers and wire-cutters
for breaking the familiar knots of habit.
And continued to her own demolition sites
whose scaffolding tested her head for heights.

iii

Navvies loomed, choking over the rubble
of guilt and anger, possessiveness and lust.
Up to the nondescript modern block;
its Divorce Registry, not listed on the board,
had a bell for entry as if for some award

to offices smelling of dirty deeds, sworn
over bibles meaninglessly. Islam?
Polyandry? Anything—rather than be handed,
over the counter, a Decree Absolute
which would set her on a well-trodden route

to isolation. Where were the mourners,
the healing ritual and headlines in the paper
about a woman acting as her own Judge
while her husband disintegrated into a respondent,
then signature? The officials kept silent.

Only the lift, going down, hummed
shamefully of failure, of a sadness meant to be
a relief in incongruous shadows of loving-cups.
Rejecting the formal, cold-blooded slaughter,
the marriage dissolved itself in the rising water.

And wild flowers, drying themselves in grass,
closed their petals into lockets for her to keep
and fill with a life's best—not for the dividing.
She walked numbly downtown with her needs,
maintaining her image in fake widow's weeds.

Restitution

I am dedicating my body now to my horse:
a chestnut mare. She will carry it proudly
through tracks lined with cow parsley, gorse,
rhyming it with her own wheel of energy.

She will understand its language of possession,
inspiration and fear; its commands in the angle
of hip or shoulder, thrust of a breast, position
of each seat bone. In reddened woods I will sit tall,

while she responds, matched to the season,
in tune with my intensity. She will lead me
past ponds studded with kingcups into the span

of Pegasus' wings, into the owl's fluted cry.
I will give her my softest hands, biggest heart
when she moulds herself to me, no asking why.

Childless Woman

You remember the children you got that you did not get
   Gwendolyn Brooks: 'The Mother'

Other people's offspring are hard to take; you
See them as miracles you never performed, try not to remember
The ones you lost from your womb: girls with the
Intense look of yours in their eyes, at play with other children
In sand pits, on roller skates, pink ribbons in their ponytails. You
Dress them in hand-smocked tana lawn frocks, pretend
   they got
Double firsts just for being themselves. The fortune-teller
   says that
Three boys, not girls, are looking out for you up there. You
Imagine them heartbreakers delivered by a stork. Even if
   you did
Shy away from hushabyes once, now you would not.
Too old to carnival into motherhood, poems are all you
   can beget.

Odd One Out

Abused child, Exbury school, the New Forest

Once three is three, two threes are six, three threes…
The twelve times' tables chorused every lunch hour
by heart in the primary school when Miss Inder went out.

Big room. Little room. The chant rising to a rap,
lips like baby birds opening and closing for food.
Hers never moved, though, under her puffy black eyes.

She had no name, no friend, her skin scabbed with weals—
noughts and crosses marked in the spaces with blood.
In the playground when older girls bounced smaller ones

up and down on their knees: *the farmer's horse
goes plod, plod, plod, the lady's horse goes trit-trot,
trit-trot, trit-trot…* she stood rigid, impaled on the fence,

expecting, maybe, to get shot by conkers of the roughest boys.
Her clothes, patched with dirt, seemed stolen from a scarecrow.
Her hair, tangled with rumours of nits, scabies, circled her

like a skipping rope never swung to rhymes. No one
saw her being dropped off or collected—was it from
the pig-swill van, by the tinker or rag-and-bone man?

When the bell clanged, and the children climbed trees
to escape the stallions sparring with each other in the lane,
she did not shift. The soles of her down-at-heel shoes

flapped against the gravel in time to the frenzied whinnies—
as if the ponies spoke her language not meant for translation
onto slate or board. Then the fatal day a police car pulled up…

six threes are eighteen, seven threes are twenty one, eight threes
are twenty four, nine threes are twenty seven, ten threes are thirty…
And Miss Inder returned, strict as a stick, to announce her gone.

Dirty Old Men of Dublin

My childhood was full of them: dirty old men
charming snakes from opened flies. One
with a pledge badge on his lapel, grandchildren
like us, so he said; another hairy as an ape
in a beach hut. The regular always carried a gun.

If we passed him on our bikes, we hitched a lift back
in the bread van, in the wake of rabbits skinned.
Others hid in the grounds of derelict houses,
cultivating themselves in frames, under glass,
or creeping under creepers, silent as guards.

We glimpsed them from secret platforms in trees
or as we cut our wrists scaling walls of trespass.
We knew no more about men than cross-pollination
and, with cow parsley veils over our faces,
we dared each other approach their beckoning fingers.

Slimy and red-veined, they seemed mere mock-ups
from compendiums, necessary for our adventures
out of bounds. We saw one playing with long grass
as if making a bow for the fiddle of a malingerer.
On a slab of concrete he sat, watching us

seesawing over foundations of a new estate—
on a plank and barrel, the child on top jumping off
to give the other a bump—into his arms. Rough
getting jolted hard enough to see stars and hear choirs
of angels pronounce a place without these odd men.

With the police-force of the Church behind us, we began
to fluff our lines in their defence before the Gardaí.
If the old men had repressed urges, then so did we.
They sit in our psyches now, the sad old men,
potential harm-doers, in subtle delineations often

of word or thought, not graphically translated
into action. We cannot disown their proclivities.
With masks instead of veils over our faces, we start
to burrow under truths, under feelings, under whatever
is easiest not to confront—as if we are copying them

from a remove, under ivy and convolvulus creepers.
In our case, they stressed sex only as the undertone it is
at every age, in every life. Yet while sirens wail,
judges' wigs curl and keys clink in locks—
who would drop the charges and believe us?

Return of the Drag Queens

Drag-queen storytellers are hoping to go into Bristol primary schools to add some sparkle to lessons—and overcome a few ingrained social prejudices to boot.

Times Educational Supplement, 23 June, 2017

We knew them back then: drag queens
in pantomime, with deep cleavages,
bouffant wigs, sequins and feather boas,

on heels high, almost, as stilts. Their voices—
bawdy, bass—mocked any proper lady's
or dame's. How risqué they were popping

their suspenders, tightening their corsets,
with a flash of an inner thigh. Remote
as ogres and monsters in fairy tales—

they helped us handle fears and traumas;
didn't expect us to cope with their reality.
Yet now they are sashaying from theatres

and music halls, faded cross-dressers
as they cross old boundaries, cross-hatching
traditional story books, before inscribing

new themes: boy princesses in dresses
skin-tight, girl kings with moustaches.'
They cross-stitch into their performances

tots too young, even, for rôles at Christmas
in live cribs. Like them, back then, we
were innocent of prejudiced etymologies.

As girls we acted in *Ten Little Nigger Boys*
in the village hall, and counted backwards
with dread as we dropped down until

'there were none'. With playgrounds full
of tomboys and sissies, and hermaphrodites
as imaginary friends, we didn't need lessons

in skewered genders even if we defined boys
by their crossbars on bikes, girls by tutus,
blocked satin toes. The drag queens are back,

stripping blues and pinks from nurseries,
encouraging same-sex crushes before their time.
While their false eyelashes sweep from floors

of classrooms the ladybirds and caterpillars
collected in matchboxes, we re-invent
cat-calls and wolf-whistles to usher them out.

Ivy Leaves

His hands were shaped into ivy leaves
that climbed up the tree, camouflage
for its inner rings, tickling the light.
Horse chestnut buds had given them
a stickiness which the rains could not
wash off. Touch them, he said.

He played games in the June garden,
named himself a bee, gold-striped:
a worker coming at her secret flower.
She had to open her petals, one
by one, even if it hurt. He would
make her queen of the princesses

she'd read about, would pretend
his body was a palace, hive-white.
He would paint faraway jungles
on her back if she'd take off her dress.
All the trees undressed, he said,
at the summer's end and didn't care

who was looking. His fingers turned
into bunches of sweet peas. She could
squeeze them for their scent, he said.
Bottles were waiting: red, blue,
yellow in the greenhouse, and cacti
that would make her shriek and shiver.

He pressed his face against hers.
Grafting, he called it. He did it
all the time. Only later did she recall
the earwigs and woodlice under the glass
while the green hands of ivy clung
to her nakedness and would not let go.

Plaint to Epona

Roman goddess of horses

for Coco

Epona, where were you?
Your ears, in the corn, deaf
to what the wind warned,
your prowess in fertility
not safeguarding that foal
who lived just a single day?

Epona, where were you?
No help to the bereaved mare
trying to lick back into life
the inert foal: her first—
and the proudest natural mother
the stud had ever seen?

Epona, was it deliberate:
laying that perfect dun colt
in your patera as an offering
to the gods instead of food
or wine? Surely you knew
better, your own mother a mare?

Up to us, now, to hold him
in our hearts; to frame him
like a cave-painting, primitive,
with his black dorsal stripe,
the star on his tiny dished face
leading us further than Bethlehem.

As a wild spirit stallion, stabled
elsewhere, he will grow up
to lead our souls on after-life rides—
and ensure that his dam breeds
another: like him, but a filly
named, not Earl, but Epona.

Old Retreat Notebook

Cum facent, clamant…
Cicero

A keepsake, she opens it with its yellowed pages,
its faded handwriting in the attempted italics
of a young girl on a retreat hushed as the soles
of nuns' feet, as the swish of their long veils.

Glued in are holy pictures swapped in compline
and benediction, her harrowing versions—
culled from the Passionist Father—of the stations
of the Cross, deadly sins, of vocations

for women and the wisdom of sticking to crowds
when company-keeping with boys. Stunned
with long tapers is the wax creak of candles,
dropped: the rhythmical jangle of chains

swung to release incense from silver thuribles.
Five days and five nights: the rule of silence
broken by giggles, whispers and apple-pie beds,
by ghostly Church Latin in aisle and cloister.

And then the unwritten script of the willed hush,
urgent as a siren, of the woman she became.
Her deliberate calm in domestic scenes as she battered
its shield into shape by the strength in her veins.

She held it against her breast when blood coursed,
cold, down her back during his night terrors—
not those of the Saviour under olive trees in the Garden
of Gethsemane. She tried breaking her vow,

fists against his chest, but this only intensified rows,
his physique superior. So she kept it, lips pursed,
felt pads pasted on to the undersides of her feet
enabling her to stand upright, and be taught

the supremacy of self-education by experience.
She closes the notebook and listens to where gales
run out of breath, winded, and vixens hunt
into earths their own ravening murderous cries.

In deep folds of snow, behind shockwaves,
soundlessness slips through the nuns' habits, cells,
under their exercises for self-mortification—
down its own slipways into the sanctuary of song.

Love Songs

Love songs, where are you?
Your entrails in the shy nests
of nightingales, wedged
in the throats of troubadours?

My pulse lacks your beats,
your manuscripts yellowed.

Love songs, you had a skin,
smooth and silken, to polish
mine, a rhythm to revive
the heart drained of hope.

Where are those sopranos
and tenors you hired for me?

Love songs, recall them—
even if only in snatches.
Then swell nests and throats
with silences that surpass

old strains. Tap my feet—
and sway me again into you

in the echo-chambers of woods,
on finger-boards of mountains,
under the lilt and lull of seas.
Love songs, do not desert me.

Sonnets made of Wood

To Pablo Neruda

I surrender this century to you: wooden sonnets that arise
only because you give them life.
    Pablo Neruda to Matilde Urrutia

Carve me, then, onto the smooth grain
of your sonnets—that I might be
your Matilde. I will sing up
driftwood from Atlantises planed
for you by seas inscribed already
with the tides' chopped lines. Cup
me in the curve of each cursive,
in the strung foliage alive
through the wind-played air.
You will not be her betrayer
for I have my own tools to share
work on seasoned lengths bare
as flesh, my own chisel on offer
to bevel an eternal affair.

What woman would not want to be
the sap in beeches, the resin in acajou,
amarante, her breath turning violet
the heartwood, conjuring recitals
from trunks' ridges of braille. She
would wear on her fingers rings true
as those telling the inner age of octets
in felled cocobolo dells.
Pablo, lay out for her and for me
floorboards to polish with beeswax
for the home on your lips, the melody
of copihue bells in your arms. Impart
your skills with awl, spokeshave, axe
to restore every wedge-split heart.

Love Letters

She kept them in bundles in a drawer
that wouldn't quite shut, and in a suitcase
in the attic, her father's initials inscribed

on its mildewed lid. Did he read them,
she wondered, in the small hours, praying
for her as mice skittered over the planks,

avoiding traps. Did his ghost conclude, yes,
life had been tricky for that daughter
whom he had wanted to protect—but at least

she had been treasured at times on airmail sheets
flimsy as his missal's leafs, and in the nibs
of fountain pens on Basildon Bond,

despite the complex men she seemed fated
like a magnet, to attract. On occasions
she would peep at their faded inks

which courted her in ways she had forgotten:
how her shape in the bed was missed,
even for a night; how she couldn't be lived

without, how there were arms to hold her close,
how she was a darling, darlingest darling.
When the smoke from the chimney curled

into cursives of the devil on the iron fireback,
and the cottage walls shook—without opening
drawer or case, she took refuge in those lines

which outlasted their passions, outlasted too
that desired girl-woman she had once been,
her father's initials stamped upon her heart.

Homeward Bound

Leaning from the carriage door ages after you'd gone,
I pretended that a steam train was leaping its tracks
to reach, ahead of time, the station where your dot

expanded into a battered hat, flapping trousers and eyes
about which jokes cracked themselves into lines
of hair-raising stories. On a pension, yet a tycoon

in humanity, you'd grab the luggage from my mind
before doors slammed shut and charge off to the car—
wreckless in the steam with your spectral self, despite

a war disability. My father. In railway buffets
I inspect hands warmed on teacups for yours to be
translated from the dream and I eavesdrop in case

your snippets have stayed behind to advise and entertain.
Sometimes I run the train's length, past pistons, jumping
out and back in again for it to pull away like your cortège

whistling, at empty bunkers, the heartless complexities
of absence. More often I stay put, bags uncarried
while express after express... *clickety-clack, clickety-clack...*

flashes past stops where trollies replace porters and you wait,
then clatter along with me in every tense. Taking up
your dares, I save you a seat first class on return journeys

where, having fallen asleep, or extracting life histories
from fellow passengers, you miss your station. Now,
it seems, you made up all the timetables, changed points

to your whim and confounded train spotters with names
of your old battleships on engines, instead of numbers.
Because smuts forbid your reflection in windows

and every moment is an emergency in your lack, I pull
communication cords, careless of fines, caught in your wink
behind inspectors' backs. Fumbling with a season ticket

from which distances shunt on a line whose signals redden,
I book journeys to your infinities. As you wave
from weightless platforms, anywhere is home.

Never without her

He never had to do without her.
Her smile lived in his eyes,
her presence clothed him.

Odd times when apart,
she breathed in his rhymes
scrawled on shreds of paper

that padded out his pockets.
He shaped her in his shout:
hand cupped to his mouth—

Kath, Kath. Mavourneen.
Through streets, esplanades,
night lights, her tall figure

echoed to his need, fell in
with his step. Then back.
He never had to do without her.

We had to do without him
histories ago. When the car
knocked him down, his lips

stiffened into the call of her name,
the pleasure-boat he had planned
to captain for trips with her

around his body and heart
drawn up forever alongside her
in his broken arms' harbour—

flags all drooped at half-mast.
We have had to do without her.
And make-do now with her face

reflected still in his monocle,
with his love for her in old songs
crooning in his West Cork blood:

Believe me if all those endearing
young charms, Now the day is over...
His fiddle trembles in its case

as we chime in with him:
...soon I'll be sailing far across
the sea. O please remember me!

The Man who killed my Father

I never gave you a name, or face.
I knew you were young as me and sorry,
very sorry, not your fault at all.
He was always reckless, my father.

I knew you were young as me and sorry.
Running across roads in front of the traffic,
he was always reckless, my father.
He held up buses like a pretend policeman,

danced the lanes in front of the traffic.
Or sat me at the wheel of his Austin,
rules to the wind, flouting policemen,
egging me on to steer, steer—

to spin the Casino wheel of his Austin,
in a race with the vehicle in front, ready
for take-off. My learner hands steered
up and down potholed switchbacks,

racing speed itself—not at all ready
for you to appear on his horizon—
to steal the ups from fate's switchbacks:
a stranger with no idea that morning

you would sever his horizon
and end the world by running over a man.
You couldn't help being you that morning.
At first I wanted to kill you, too,

end your world as you'd run over a man,
and crush with a bulldozer your Volkswagen.
Yes, I wanted to kill you, too,
for daring to live on past that fatal dawn,

polishing your undented Volkswagen.
Years I have had to live with the break—
true, you had no choice that fatal dawn—
in every bone of his, every missed beat...

Years I have been marked by the break
in a heart, the gap in every song,
trying to set his broken bones, re-start the beat
and to imagine him brushing his teeth

a second longer so the gap in every song
might sing again, the awful coincidence
of timing be ground to nothing by his teeth
and you rev up through playful shadows,

penance done for the one-off coincidence.
Older than he was now, we share
sunlight's slow bleach of that black shadow.
More than sorry, not your fault at all.

The Walking stick

When we parted, my husband took it from my mother's
        house—
with its twisted wood, its handle a dragon's grooved head,
jammed in its mouth what looked like a stone or ball.

I never queried its significance: just knew it had been made
by an ageless sage who had never before seen a white man
two thousand miles in the interior of China. He carved it

in front of my father, an expert in the Yangtze's currents,
rapids, gorges as he navigated its snaking length, up
and down, past bamboos, willows, lotus blossom, Dove trees,

playing with white-flag dolphins when they chose to appear,
deciphering the ideographs written by the wind on water.
I wonder now if that longago husband simply stored it

in a corner; if his son when a child conjured silken colours
of ancient and new Oriental worlds at his every poke,
summoned onto his screen naga-queens dressed in the lace

of rain-trees' leaves, hidden from the enemy bird, the Garuda.
While that husband leans on it between workouts, its ball
clamped, my ghost father and sage grab it back

to reveal the jewel it is that grants all desires, the mani
of the mystic, the moon-pearl which lightens the deepest nights.
I twirl and twirl it like a majorette dancing on the stars.

Grey... and the poet

Grey the ocelot fur she lay upon
in thigh-high boots, leather corset,
flogging him in the small hours
while, on all fours, he yelped for more.

Grey as ashes her hands, her po-face
as she tied him to the bed head, then
went about her business, preparing
tawses and nails for a St Andrews cross.

Grey her lips smeared with insults—
a wise old woman's, a virgin's, whore's—
as she polished chains, opening the door
of her steel cage, next on the list for him.

Grey the walls of her dungeon
in which she laid out the masks
worn by her: of Enterpe, Calliope, Thalia.
while she perched on his shoulder.

Grey she had turned them in dresses
printed with lines pinched to death
by her forceps on the point of delivery.
Her delight: to play blind man's buff—

grey the light—with passions
he thought needed to be goaded
into expression by enslavement,
not by soft enticements of the Muses.

Grey his own skin he lay upon
stripped of his skeleton that squirmed still
from subjection, pages silenced from
the clamps and pegs of his failed creation.

Piano Player

Play through me gently with the best of yourself
as long ago when, a young bride and groom,
we swayed to your pub favourites, jazz

and honky-tonk. We sang, also, in harmony,
to your fingers which flew of their own accord
over ivories, fluent, sure of their dexterity.

Play through me sadly, summoning the wild roses
on pergolas, the logs flaming into rainbow colours
granted fleetingly by grace—and forget the rest:

those hammers of Thoth struck against our skins
from warped strings, the chords reluctant to resolve
which banged off keys, disturbed in their din.

Play through me by ear, still, that I might admire
your accomplishment while I practise haltingly
from manuscripts you did not need, yellowed now,

corners torn from too many turnings in lessons:
preludes, waltzes, sonatas receding into a silence
that stuns metronomes, inhibits expression.

Play through me by heart. As reflections re-appear
in the mahogany, let me sway once more
to your medley, caught in the octaves of gorse-light

spanned by your hands. Tuners under the lid
muffle old time-signatures, lock us out from performing
duets from distances, *presto*, as time's recitative bids.

Play through me gently, sadly, by ear and by heart,
composing a counterpoint to melodies of wind,
flock, wave for the gaps on staves of our two parts.

His Second Wife

Facebook 1

She has befriended me on Facebook.
I have to say I like her sense of fun,
her love of her son and grandchildren,

I am ashamed to resent her 'pilfering':
not so much the tickets first class,
once mine, when I trod over glass,

the luxury hotels dream edifices now,
the bride I used to be on my knees
to her man who gagged the banshees

when I left… It's more in the scenes
on vacation from abroad she puts online:
Killiney hill I once called mine—

that granite chair from the Famine
I wished upon; in each framed photo
of Dalkey Island, the Vico,

Killiney Bay with its smooth ribbon
of sand, tide out, I galloped around
the Lead Mines' tracks, the pony sound..

She publicises them all on screen:
Bulloch and Coliemore harbours
under a sky Marian blue; our oars

shipped still in their rain-prinked calms
which print our shrimp nets, skinny dips,
goose pimples in memory's edited clips.

Yet she has a right to each touchstone,
each bygone vista that suddenly nears.
No one can own a place that appears

when in it— then disappears.
Our loving-cup—buried in the years—
toasts the two of them: three cheers.

Facebook 2

There she is again, proud deportment
beside her man: the perfect couple
at a College reunion; on high table,
then in Front Square. How meek
he looks tucked in against her
in his well-pressed tails, his hair
that he claimed turned suddenly white
when I left him still thick on his head.
I wonder if they share a sleigh bed—

and if he recalls a similar photo
snapped by his mother's Brownie Box
on graduation day: mortar boards
and gowns, black and white, smiles
from our two young faces washed
with hope. Click, click…memory prompts
like the Cunard liner, the QE2,
to mark this occasion, it seems,
moored strategically in Dublin Bay—

a mere cruise ship now—to take him
back, back to the time, a bottle broken
over its prow, we sailed in it
to the Brave New World: husband
and wife that he'd slapped on the face

the day before, handkerchiefs waved
in Cobh, emigrants first class. There
in front of Howth Head it swanks,
fit for the two of them to indulge

in its menus long as an arm, spot prizes
on dance floors, the years up to their tricks:
mellowing him into a dependence,
uptight no longer, anger all calmed?
I look again. Her post has sunk
below my screen, sunk out of sight,
as if never there. And I ask myself
who would I have been had I stayed
with him, upright like her? Or a shade?

All my long-gone horses

All the long gone darlings
Sylvia Plath's 'All the Dead Dears'

They walk along with me, side by side:
my horses of a lifetime: a chestnut, grey,
skewbald, two dark browns, a bright bay,
palomino, nuzzling, whickering at me
to take them all, bare-back, for a ride.

In the switchback fields they grazed
I know each hump, sett, each fox's run,
which holly bush they chose for protection
in easterly blasts, which branches in summer
formed canopies against flies as the sun blazed.

I descend the slopes as if I have hooves,
feel the firmer sandy ground they found
for galloping down to a halt, and around
over the gully, bucking, blood up, or spooking,
tails high, at twigs or leaves on the move.

I treasure, still, each pothole in the clay
their thunderous charge made as they came
to my call. Their graceful ghosts, wild and tame,
leap the five-bar gates of Time beyond hedge
and fence, yet, ears pricked, choose to stay

where I have outlived them. My herd, they stand,
head to tail, tail to head, in a circle around me
while I blow into their nostrils, rhythmically
in, out—then scratch their withers, crests, rumps.
I want them to take carrots again from my hand;

to pick blackberries delicately from brambles.
I crave to soak sugar-beet for them in frozen days,
to fill their mangers with the sweetest soft hay.
O to be trampled upon rather than to stare
into the real emptinesses of thistle-blown air.

His mother

She buffed his words with her best Lavender polish
and hung them like horse brasses from the sunbeams
that stole from black clouds into the front room.

In the wedding photograph, the white bride I was
stood on the mantelpiece; his certificates for sport
and academic prowess papered the walls with pride.

Though attending Mass no longer on Sundays—
married to a protestant, she kept bottles of holy water
in her handbag to sprinkle on whatever went out of tune.

She trimmed herself for her son when he called her
plump, her long slim legs ready always to dance,
yet shying away from table-tops, stage floors.

Did she know about the pressures he put on himself,
a perfectionist? Wish he had given in to his whim
of farming pigs on a Wicklow mountainside,

his earthed self to the fore, not jet-setting
with mandarins, appearing to her like a vision
every home-leave when, up an octave, her voice

spun him into the wonder boy she had given birth to.
Down the years when I didn't know her, I knew
in my bones she saved for me feathered nests,

a lucky horse shoe, a metronome. To this day, I keep
in my bag a Saint Christopher travelling card from her
for when I lived mid-flight in planes about to crash.

From the other side, now, she smiles, a blusher
on her high cheekbones, in the velvet dress dyed
with sunsets I gave her that vanished time ago.

I see her slip into tap shoes and ballroom courts never hers
when here, offering new rhythms in her skirt's sway—
unwitting choreographer of my buckled, spent heart.

The Walk from Louisburgh to Delphi Lodge

Wind-warped we slithered over the hard gums
of a region whose crooked, impacted teeth of marble
ground over a territory famished, still, for growth.
Only rhododendrons, potentilla, Irish Spurge

and mombresia had escaped the walled gardens
of a demesne to mock, in a decorative frieze,
pot-holed bohreens hacked out for the transportation

of fodder. Echoes of eight hundred blistered, bare,
staggering feet pattered too light a rhythm
to the driving rain which pelted down its grave-stones.
We could but watch for spectral skeletons

to wave their rags and threads, to rattle a gold coin
from a stocking, a cloak, or to bribe with geese: as if
we were not witnesses but paid Vice-Guardians.

With a deserved guilt, we followed a fraction
of the trudge from Louisburgh to Delphi Lodge.
We forbade ourselves to wade in the Glankeen River
under toppling hills, to dream of wild salmon

stolen by the Colonel and the English gentleman
whose barred Georgian door caused the cottiers
to die where they stood, faster than by any gun.

A few stick-figure girls: *Catherine Grady*,
Mary McHale, Honor Dillon possessed names
at least that surfaced from anonymous sandbanks
and sloughs to be engraved upon the coffins

of their thoughts. Such twisted dominion
stole the heart out of the people more than fears
of granite jaws clamped over the bitter vision.

From behind curtains

Erin Pizzey's Shelter for Women,
2 Belmont Place, Chiswick, founded 1971

From behind curtains they creep,
hunched mostly, hands over their faces
to avoid being recognised, like criminals

rather than victims. Some have children
trailing, or babies at the breast; others
hug the walls, ashamed of their own shadows

or cling to hot water bottles for comfort.
Immigrants of a different kind, from terror
in their own rooms, skin-scarred, scarred

within, most have bruises and scratches
that look tattooed on, eyes hollow and staring.
Open their bags and you will not find

the expected addictions to storm and calm,
histories of abusive parents, though many lose
their voices, forced into Munch's silent scream.

Some hands tremble still as if with palsy,
some breaths do not breathe; others fumble
for valiums or rosaries to give them courage

here and acknowledge there will be
no more going back to the partner when his fit
of rage is over and sex offers its cheap relief.

From behind curtains they creep, blaming
themselves, craving still to back out
and pretend nothing will ever again go wrong .

This—such a final statement that will strip them
of what they know, will lose them income, a home,
circles of friends. From mansions, flats and slums

they do their best to start carrying their worlds
upside down on their heads, bearings lost—
then creep back behind the curtains' smooth swish.

Stalker

I am being stalked by a hundred-headed hydra
with venomous breath and blood, his scent deadly.

When I glimpse him behind curtains, at the mirror,
he tries to catch my eye, then climbs over
the naked parts of myself that I numb—like ivy.

His lids will not close while he lurks in the curve
of tomcats' silken tails, in my shadow.

In black felt hats of countless uncaught gangsters
he poses, a step behind me always, before vanishing
into his own lopsided grin. In my kitchen window

I catch a flash of him. Or he crouches in the shower,
dampens fires, ensures the piano stays out of tune.

He breathes heavily through the Devil's snout
inside the Tower of Babel, filling it with a chorus
of shrieks that he injects into my head, as opportune

with the Tarot cards I pick as when at arm's length.
At each creak of a door or rustle of a leaf, I know

he is patrolling the undergrowth, and shimmying
up and down drainpipes. His feet rattle the gravel
with a foxtrot: *slow, slow, quickquick slow* ...

as he waits for the chance to tread on my toes.
I ask angel guardians to clamp onto his pulled faces

their wings, then to stalk him along the paths
in my psyche to sacrosanct places, until
their blasts of hosannas reduce him to a space.

Woman of an Age

Britain has one of the worst records in Europe on age discrimination
The Observer

They are making you nameless, having to prove
your identity on the phone to insurance companies,
banks, by the mileage you have clocked up

when your age is like a swearword you try to forget.
You want to tell them to mind their own business,
stop forcing you into a straitjacket, as if you never had

a past, any youth, and preserve, still, a shy glint
of former Maytimes in your eyes. You look
on the bright side; think at last you are managing

to live in the present, even if in a fixed stagnancy,
not in the fluid instant you tried, always, to grasp.
In it shop assistants start to call you *love, dearie, darlin,*

ask if you want the lad stacking the shelves to carry
your lightweight bags to the car. In the ticket office,
the woman presumes you have concessions, the tone

in her voice insistent, as if she has found you out,
and is ticking you off for not filling out the form
of your final admission. Her eyebrows rise at your request

for an ordinary day return. You strut along the platform
in skinny jeans, as if a vibrant part, still, of the workforce,
nothing to do with you: the dump of the retired. In rush hour,

standing, you convince yourself the commuter
offering his seat is chivalrous, old-school, and you thank him
with a determinedly girlish smile. Back home you hide

the letter offering a fuel allowance; peer into mirrors
with eyesight better than any face-cream at smoothing lines,
sun damage, age spots, thread veins. Candlelight

too performs its facelifts—so you remove light bulbs
in the pretence that you are going green. When wolfwhistles
assail you, you are thrilled not to be 'past it'—and keep

under your hat that you can recall, just, flying boats, horses
delivering coal, groceries, dashboards on cars, steam trains.
As you help uphill all the old fogeys and dodderers

younger probably than yourself, you cling to the fact
that the heart never grows old, that inside yourself you
haven't changed. But they lie in wait—with their chains.

Painted Lady

Never a permanent resident,
I live everywhere, choosing disturbed
and open areas to host my complexities.

Gardens, vacant lots, set-aside fields,
dunes and dumps let me grace them
with the imprints I bear—of my travels:

the heat rising like a shimmer off piazzas
in an Africa shaped by drum-beats on skin;
patchwork pieces cut from black burkahs

of shy-eyed Arabian and Indian women
whose faces and bodies, like mine, remain
obscured, our wing-span that of angels.

No one knows how, in my migrations
from cacti sculptures in dry Mexican deserts,
I let ghosts of Aztecs trace on me the patterns

in orange, brown and white of their mandalas,
fill my dreams with struggles for completeness.
My eyes, in summer, change from black

to the blue in skies which show me off
as a daring acrobatic flyer, fragile enough still
for high pressure systems. Clockwise winds

and anticyclones dictate which destinations
will offer me their thistles, hollyhocks, mallow;
which ironweed, blazing star, red clover and privet

will tempt me with nectar; which flowerheads
on hedge-mustard beds in the pollen-filled air
will be alive with me. Sometimes I surge northwards

with hundreds of my reflections. Tapping out
the row of small black dots on my dorsal hindwing,
I practise a morse code that reveals the secrets

of why I distribute myself so widely, why—never
a permanent resident in disturbed and open areas—
I offer only a painted moment as redemption.

Philomel

Philomel—

Was it so terrible what you underwent
that you could not recover your song
stolen by the male that did you wrong?

No tongue, sharp or flat, no decibel
to borrow from the wind in the woods
of your perches, no note to swell—

Philomel.

Silenced forever, how can you bear
to listen to arias from the virtuosos
of your kind, piercing, pure—and know

from the thicket where your shyness hides
your talent far surpasses what you hear,
yet stays day and night unappreciated inside?

Philomel—

forget how you were raped and torn
in yellowed deserts and spiked downland dells,
how, never out of tune, you were accused

of croaking in a choir, the conductor's baton
against your throat, as blackcaps and warblers
whistled your name. Even when gone—

Philomel—

in your plain brown body, a *laide-belle*,
may you find cellos, tongues, feathered flutes
for the undertones winged on your spell.

Rock Horses

For the battered women I round up
from hillsides the herd that can never die:

white stallions from stone and bronze ages.
I exercise their stiffened limbs, take them

to smithies to be shod with the moon's crescents.
From Uffington, Alton Barnes, Westbury, Hackpen

they loom, backs dipped into hammocks
for the battered women who, when mounted,

survey countries and oceans not on any map,
then carve their initials for luck on steaming flanks.

Too large to be measured by hands, at sunset
the horses disappear into grass on angled downs.

The battered women dream of their crests
and waterfalling tails as they are carried through malls

to forts where they start again to shape new lives,
rockabye rocked by the herd until kingdom come.

The angels keep

The angels keep their ancient places;
Turn but a stone, and start a wing!
Francis Thompson, *The Kingdom of God*

For the children killed in Manchester, May 22, 2017

The angels keep their ancient places.
Turn but a stone, and start a wing.
See their stolen childhood faces,
an iPhone, a hairband covered in bling.

The angels hold them in new spaces.
dress them in clouds as they swing
from prayers, tying their sneakers' laces,
each one a popstar now who sings.

The angels arrange three-legged races,
invite them to cart-wheel in a ring.
They will shower us with graces
if we turn but a stone and start a wing.

Rest, young lady

Chagall to Sarah d'Avigdor-Goldsmid

All Saints Chapel, Tudeley

Summer's lease hath all too short a date.
Shakespeare, Sonnet 18

Rest, young lady, in the light I give you.
It has no side or lid, just a shaped surface
to keep you safe in all the time that was
and will be. Accustomed already to the glass

of the sea on that calm, foggy night, you
will hear the song of the diamond as I trace
your story, cutting it with watercolours
and gouache into leaded zones that trespass

like shafts of grace on aisle, chancel, pew.
How drawn I was to you, bladderwrack-bound,
to your Christian mother, father the Hasidic Jew.

In their mansion silhouetted above the chapel,
what did they know of Boreas's random gust,
the dinghy upturned, stars unread, the knell?

Rest, young lady, over those jigsawed shadows
of wrecks—while upended horizons jousted
for your hand. The Channel's fittest horses

which could have saved you stood in shallows,
denied the gales from Dungeness to Beachy Head
veering under their hooves into hurricane force.

My fingers and brush-tips have scratched lines
at eye-level on that east window, to compose
a lullaby in gradations of blues that rock
your body; your mother cradles you, a child—

long before your drowning; a friend pines,
the red mare is there for you to ride, and a cross
with a ladder to climb from fathom, fin, bedrock.
No crown of thorns, black-cloaked Boreas reviled

when, from the graveyard, he batters the glass,
his bloat-cheeks, punctured, shrivel into grass.

Sarola

Charmer of charms, twister of ages and places,
you walk still as if with a water pitcher on your head,
push back the sticks and sickles they hit you with,

pull the boots off the husbands who kick you
in your pregnant belly, the impression of their feet
deforming the foetus into a concave kidney bean.

Charmer of charms, you hide in the bougainvillea.
Fine-boned still, your plait, now white, is the long hand
of a clock that tells no hours, the slap-slap of dung cakes

against a wall what you time your life to. Long gone
into a lily pond the dowries of water buffaloes,
snakeskins and watches that you didn't have…

Charmer of charms, your sieves now tambourines
have forgotten the rice they separated from stones
and, upended, serve as weapons while you try

to fight back the slave labour they force on you,
no matter what caste: Gurung, Chhetri, Brahmin—
thin as a joss stick in your downtrodden gender.

Charmer of charms, where are you these days?
Somewhere along the Ganges, applying strips
of paw-paw to old skin wounds, still having to eat

off your husband's dinner plate once he has finished,
bound by your hair that he pulls into elongated strands?
Do you remember the missionaries hawking bibles

who pretended to donate scripts for languages
that had no script, and Hindu relations locking
the converted into their sheds as traitors,

no food, no water, then, knives out, killing them?
Are you, like the others, not daring to tell
of the atrocities against you: how you are set on fire—

Charmer of charms—called a witch, tired of having
to greet your husband and in-laws upon waking,
forbidden to set foot in mosques, temples, stupas,

your hand-stitched prayer mats torn up. Sarola, maybe
you are reincarnated into every one of these women,
even those urbanised who are locked up in apartments.

Your shadows mass along the Ring Road,
faces mirrored in puddles of diesel oil: all
charmers of charms, too many to count and save.

Epilogue: When all is said and done

… and yet when all is said
It was the dream itself enchanted me.
Yeats' 'The Circus Animals' Desertion'

When all is said and done, down long corridors
of time, portraits of the selves you have become
hang, faceless, beside mine that are turned
to the wall. I no longer know by heart the voice
echoing in the accents—surely not yours—
of a cowboy, yank, every hint gone, in the scrum
for identity, of the original Irish you spurned
once for the adopted Englishness of your choice.

My privilege, now, to pick out the best of you.
Fond of that lad, fading to a ghost, who spun
on his bike through spinneys of wild garlic
and watched me, on pavements we both knew,
hopscotch over whatever would be said and done— .
I return you—part-person, part-place—to myth.

The Erl King's Shroud

Den Erlen Konig mit Kron' und schweif
  Goethe/Schubert

A recitative for piano and voices

The shadow is a moral problem that challenges the whole ego-personality, for no one can become conscious of the shadow without considerable moral effort. To become conscious of it involves recognizing the dark aspects of the personality as present and real. This act is the essential condition for any kind of self-knowledge.
  C. G. Jung *Aion* (1951). CW 9, Part II: P.14

The Erl King, my love, see he rides near
in the highest winds between old and new years
with crown and sceptre and snow-white shroud...
his horse champing edges of the darkest cloud.

The Erl King he hovers, hunting, wild—
after maiden, woman, manikin and child.....
his ebony night-mare paws the hard ground,
more lunar than solar, ears pinned back
as it rides those bed-fellows sleeping sound.

　　　The Erl King he beckons, like a knight in arms,
　　　she his adopted daughter he will keep from harm.

　　　He will teach her to shimmy, then pole-dance at night,
　　　lulling men with pop-songs to give them delight.

See his night mare, my love, lining her nest
in the hollow of the yew with her long fetlock hairs
and feathers of buzzards snatched from the air.
She stamps on the jaw-bones of poets there,

her lips bloodied from their tangled entrails,
their words deleted by her shoes' loosened nails.

> She grooms the horses
> until she sees herself
> mirrored in their coats
> through all her ages.
> She plaits her hair into
> their long, unpulled manes,
> looks out of their eyes.
> Through their ears—
> whose shifting angles
> predict storms—
> she hears earth tremors,
> the clap of taffeta wings.
> Their whinnies orchestrate
> her days as she cares
> for them and they care for her,
> instinctive in reciprocity.
> A head on each of her shoulders,
> they speak to her
> with deep breaths that
> she breathes deeply back.
> Their front hooves
> are her own small feet.

For his daughters the Erl King has fashioned
dresses from the yards of every lover's skin.
Their twirls, swirls and flounces hurt her within.

From the hammers of the polished boudoir grand
he has stripped the green felt, banged down the lid,
trapping fingers of virtuosos who must do as he bids.

She can only sit tight, ears plugged, head bowed,
while his words box her, and he shoves her
between his broken teeth to mangle her into a shroud.

    Nothing is sacred: myths are reversed:
    malefactors who run away from themselves

    are rounded up in Sodom and Gomorrah:
    words are not flesh, nor flesh word.

    Gagged orators inspect Bedlam, slapping
    rhetorical devices over nonsense-crazed walls.

    Bluebeard, now bald, unlocks all his wives.
    In Hades, archangels store, under broken wings,

    the epicentres of earthquakes, while rivers coil
    and hiss and twist into unconscious forms.

Grating and hushing,
    hushing and grating,
the sea takes back
    as a mast for drowned sailors
the cross on which he hung her,
    nails shoes
onto its fastest hurdling horses.

        The blacksmith rasps the hooves,
        re-fits the shoes to balance the feet.
        Into his leather apron drop nails
        from the sky he has bought as stars.

        God of the ungodly, Thor comes
        with his bolts, victories and defeats
        to cut back the wall of the sky
        and hammer onto it the earth,

filing smooth the heads of stars.
The earth-shod sky clatters to the beat
of storms over ages of Vikings,
Celts and giants, through light years

that have no dates to where blacksmiths
put away their anvils, cool the heat
of furnaces bending iron and leave
horses to dance along concrete roads.

The Erl King predicted it: how she would die.
Turning round on her horse as she egged it on,
his stare, ice-blue, would cut her in half,
his smile twist at the profanities scrawled
as endearments on the crows-feet at his eyes,
the corpse of her self squirm, alive, in his lies.

The Erl King predicted it. Slower than slow
he would relegate old intimacies
to eunuchs' cells, force her to her forgo
favours of courting looks and honouring hands.
Then mount his twelve-bore gun, her foe,
directing it between her legs. Ready. Steady. Go.

Chiron the centaur, wounded-healer,
healing-wounder berates knackers
who take away lives before they are up;
berates him, too, for turning into
the black-jack man in a wide sombrero,
circular ear-rings dangling as he moves in her
recurrent nightmares; allots him the Labour
of mucking out the Augean Stables
through all the time before and to come.

She is banishing the babblings of bitches,
the Erl King's daughters, who dip
into ink their besoms and appear
with burnt-out letters, defunct spells
and biddings for her to appear
with him: between old and new years.

As they belly-dance through her past,
hand-cuffing her with bangles too tarnished
to attract, she bolts the doors
of her open heart lest they bag up her days
with their jealousies, then besiege
her territory to carry off love's vestiges.

She wants bouquets never sniffed by them
and silver bracelets malleable enough to fit
around girths of worlds freshly discovered.
She is bracing herself for their encroachments,
for shadows of the Erl King's daughters to take
root in trees no longer the winds' flutes.

Someone else is panting through him,
drawing tight his lips into the caricature
of a kiss, forking his tongue to cancel
her gender…The jut of a cheekbone, bead
of sweat on a brow, and she is shapeless,
wrapped in the cling-film of an escaped offender.

She cannot look the horses in the eye,
so great is the travesty he suggests,
this black-jack man: of shooting them.
She cannot look him in the eye, either.
As if in a laughing hall of mirrors

her reflection appears now in their coats
polished by her finer memories.
She strokes their bodies unlike how, once,
he tried to stroke hers, talks to them as usual,
withholding from them his terrible command.

Magpies ride them: back-packers, one
for sorrow, two for sorrow, three for sorrow,
never for joy, their white patches blackening
till they are black as ravens: black omens
of doom.

He wants each willow tree to form
into himself, the Erl King, whose badger-bite locks,
whose insults are antidotes that pierce and sting...

Before she met him, she knew him
as the rustler in her dream who polished
his twelve-bore gun and pointed it

between the horses' trusting eyes.
How they slumped, the shine gone
from their coats, no pits dug for burial.

Another time he had come with vials
full of ragwort and yew berries to stuff
into their mouths, ignoring the freeze-marks

branded on their backs, opening gates
for them to gallop to their deaths
on motorways. In no need of them.

Before she met him, she knew him
in her dream. But she had saved them,
the horses, leading them over muckheaps

and downland to low, thatched stables
with deep straw beds, forbidding them
to whicker, snort, stale or whinny.

The Erl King, my love, he hands out seismic shocks.
His quakes, suicide bombers and waves ravage
innocent kingdoms, topple high-rise blocks…

And now he hides behind her curtain,
shakes his shroud out like a white sheet
fresh-dry from the wash; folds it in two,
in four, in eight and sixteen, then slips it
into the crack between the dark in her room
and the dark in her mind. His whiteness
is a shade of black. Blacker than black.

She wills herself away on an archangel's wing
in formation with her faithful flying horses

over seas and countries which have no names
where moons dance naked on request

and the sun is a prayer-flag; where rishis
of monks from icy summits cancel

the Erl King's rule, and she can again be wild,
her voice anyone's: man, woman or child.

She wants to shed the shroud of the Erl King,
who, whispering low in her ear, makes out
it is the shroud of her self, of her seven skins.

He is only, my love, the wind blowing wild,
colouring the crackling leaves for every single child.
His hovering form, my love, is the hollow willow tree:
a secret hushed hiding-place for you and for me.

I know, though, my love, his icy grasp will kill
the part-children we all are, subjugated to his will.
His crown, crooked sceptre and snow-white shroud
forbid me to curse him. But I do: out loud.

Her horses jump her walls of fire,
but they refuse his walls every time.

They set each other's manes alight
with their breath, their hooves

defining boundaries that do not enclose,
warding off sorcery. They protect her

from Wodan who returns to make her
his wind-bride as he gallops towards her

in the storm of her own emotions.
But they cannot keep her from ways

bashed out nightly by the Erl King.
The sea is their cradle, yet the lullaby

of the moon moves through their gait,
and sings neither to her nor to him.

Ways of the Erl King,
galloping, galloping

Is there a place where cocksfoot,
rye, and meadow fescues
grow from desert sands, where
hoofbeats and heartbeats are one,
where words serve as steps
in the line-dances of every Muse,
pulled from tone-rows of the daughters
the Erl King harps upon?

And so she journeys without travelling:
on the back of Pegasus who wings her
over to her paternal land, above ways
of sinners who cut bare penitential feet
on jagged stones, ill-equipped for the incline.

And so she is winged above clipped wings
of piety, above a sky that the faithful rip
into insurance tickets for a manmade heaven,
where irreligious crosses of cormorants dry
in the air for essentials of flight, not guilt or fear.

And so, on her command, Pegasus paws,
petitioning the seldom sun to stop pouring
grace over a race long lost to superstition;
to twist streams into silver snakes returned
from banishment, refuting Patrick's miracle.

And so Pegasus neighs her words to winds
that have whistled too long through heresies
carried in beaks through the bent trees' armoury,
winding prayers around statues and shrines.
And she is winged within wings, in wings that fly

on wings as Pegasus gives her a new ground level
for her travelling without journeying, journeying
without travelling: une Voyage à Cythère
upon which even a thought can be a pilgrimage
for the resting of a body, heart and mind.

Herakles managed it: the impossible—
cleaning the stables of Augeas
without exertion in a single day
by charming a river, maybe
to snake off course and run like mercury

through his veins before being flushed
across the deep-littered herring-bone floors.

She runs the River Lethe over different floors
in her mind, willing it to dump
into oblivion the soiled bedding, to direct
her senses beyond the world of space
and time where she could lose trace
of her Self, knower and known at last one.
But the Lethe won't let her forget its flow.

Herakles managed it: the impossible.
Hiring a high wind to round up the herd
of Diomedes' horses which ate human flesh,
he stood in their midst, hypnotising them
with whispers while he muzzled them,
then drove them against the odds to his brother
the king who had ordained the tasks.

> *It might eat us, my love, the Erl King's ebony horse,*
> *bred by Diomedes for this cross-country course.*
> *His crown and sceptre and snow white shroud*
> *are certainly no emblems in a passing cloud.*

There is a way after the leap in the dark,
the leap of trust and surrender, behind veils—

time, place and appearance stripped away
until there is no more I and You, he and she,

no more Erl Kings, demons in our psyches,
no more Bluebeards jangling their keys.

There is a way after crucifixions by mind and word,
where the heart has an all-seeing eye,

the unsaid makes saying slight
and the mind beats as a pulse in the silent desert.

There is a way in the present only when the world
of time touches the eternity into which angels peer.

The four horses of the Apocalypse
of Death, Famine, Pestilence and War
have jumped into the fields. Snorting,
biting and kicking, they gallop about,
establishing their pecking order.

The black horse of Death is rearing up
into the sky, head of the herd now
as he bucks the Erl King off his back.
And a winged horse appears, saddled
with good Fortune and the Book of Law.

> I bring to you the horses broken in by me
> without force, without bits in their mouths.
> I taught them voice commands, water music.
> Every shift of my body they learn,
> sensitive to my hands' give, take and turn
> while they transport me smoothly
> to the cloud-steeds of the Valkyries.

Through the dusk a mare emerges, eight-legged,
from the fey acreage between life and death: led

by an old, one-eyed man in a cloak, accompanied
by ravens that run and wolves that fly. Carried

under his right arm, the severed head of the Erl King
balances with another head to the left, maddening

his followers, the Beserks, who step into bear skins
to practise on the Erl King's body a vivisection.

One-eyed Wodan pats the neck of Sleipnir, his mare,
and, painting runes in blood, returns smiling to Valhalla.

> We belong still to the speed of Pegasus,
> to the flow of his mane, the grace
> of his gait. We belong to the kindliness
> in his eyes, to the pounding of his hooves
> that strike new springs of poetry.

The Erl King, even beheaded, will forever ride near
Teasing man's oldest fear of death with the fear of fear.
Yet from the choirmaster's baton hangs the frozen shroud
Melting so fast it can no longer be chorused out loud.

> Goethe created him, my love, from Teutonic myth,
> bred the horse from his blood and whipped it on
> forthwith

> to stand at stud in our psyches, blood on its sides
> from sharp studs of the Erl King on his perilous rides.

> Schubert got it fit for racing on his bass clef staves.
> His triplets gave it the rhythm to take victims to
> their graves.

> Carrying words along like riders in major and minor keys,
> tone, tune and figuration constructed the emergencies.

> Blame Goethe and Schubert for the accelerando of the duet
> whose piano and song re-create the poem for the poet.

No harpsichord, clavichord nor lute for such a Lied;
no self-effacing keyboard letting the language precede;

no drawing room gathering or aria for the shroud.
Pulled from wardrobes of folklore, it enwinds crowds.

Salsas, tangos, waltzes, foxtrots.
The daughters still dance
on jiggering staves that rot.

Salsas, tangos, waltzes, foxtrots.
The daughters still dance—
their cloven feet staccato dots.

Wild woman howls and wolves obey her.
She roars and wolves lie at her feet.

She can coil herself tighter than a snake
and extend further than the fleetest gazelle.

She is the electricity in waterfalls,
the push behind each avalanche, the leap

of spray over battered sea walls. Fearless,
she stands and waits beyond bulwarks,

beyond tired viewpoints and safe beliefs,
beyond closed doors and full stops...

She is a series of questions never to be
answered, out of reach of the fugitive

and the stay-at-home. She alone knows
how to love entirely, without reserve;

teaches how love can be devoid of touch
and reside in the hush between two breaths,

in the gaze behind the glance. As she sings up
for herself a glorified body, drumming her skin,

her heart thinks, while her mind feels.
In the lightnings which blitz the spaces

Life and Death itch in her palm into a dance
whose steps and tempo she choreographs.

Gasps, first and last, waltz on planks
of a pier over which the seas of birth

and of wrecks forever meet. Under
its rusting struts she drops her heart's silver

for mudlarks to squabble over in sands
used to sinking castles of seedy Erl kings

and their daughters. To the eldritch screech
of the owl, she embraces the shadow,

knave, child, mother and angel in herself,
then moves in to the feel of her own roundness.

> At last I am Epona,
> expert at side-saddle.
> In my navy-blue serge habit
> that cinches in my waist,
> I ride over beds of rose petals,
> revered by the Roman cavalry.
>
> And then I am Rhiannon.
> In a linseed-oiled halter,
> I carry on my back
> dead weights of dead lovers

over spiralling unholy psalters.
My mare, unbeaten on gallops,

gets coloured in by daylight,
shaped by the wind, sun-groomed.
Her mane that rays untangle
grows, golden, from my head
resurrected from the doomed
on the magical mound of Arberth.

And all my best birds sing,
awakening the dead.
In lullabies from nests
moulded by moulting coats,
they translate what I have said
until horses have bird-heads.

And I am she and she is me.
Turruling, turruling, turruling.

He was only a King

        of elves, of garden gnomes

who entrusted to the horses
the words of his corpse.

        The banshee repeated them
        in a resolving chord.

Yet in front now, not behind,

        his echo haunts homes
        broken and unbroken:

this funeral director
of burials alive

        this serial abductor
        of selves within selves

this Janus-faced
inner War-Lord.

Notes

'A Different Kind of Prison':
sadhus are wandering Hindu holy men

'Philomel': While the myth has several variations, the general depiction is that Philomel, after being raped and mutilated by her sister's husband, Tereus, obtains her revenge and is transformed into a nightingale, a migratory passerine bird native to Europe and southwest Asia. Because of the violence associated with the myth, the song of the nightingale is often depicted or interpreted as a sorrowful lament. Coincidentally, in nature, the female nightingale is mute and only the male of the species sings.

'Sarola': The 2009 Domestic Violence (Crime and Punishment) Act in Nepal, recognized for the first time that domestic violence is a crime punishable by law. However, while the act recognizes domestic violence as a crime, it contains provisions for negotiations through police offices, which seems contradictory. Although there are some laws and provisions against domestic violence, many victims are left without support mainly because of the poor mechanism to deliver support services. as well as a lack of awareness among people regarding such provisions.

'His nightmare is in the twisted hollow'...
Robert Graves writes of the hazardous nature of the poetic vocation:
'The Night Mare is one of the cruellest aspects of the White Goddess. Her nests, when one comes across them in dreams, lodged in rock-clefts or the branches of enormous hollow

★

For a performance with music:

'The Erl King's Shroud'
Lines in italics are to be recited (sung) to the original 'Erl Konig' music.

Tunes of 'Golden Slumbers kiss your eyes'...
'We will rock you, rock you, rock you' (from the carol)
'Hushabye baby upon the treetop'
'Roses whisper goodnight' (Brahms' lullaby)
to be woven throughout up until 'The Erl King's Shroud', sometimes in between poems, sometimes underneath the recited poems.

Nepalese music around the Kathmandu poems
American Indian flute music around Portrait: Red Indian

Tune of 'Come back to Erin' to be played around the Pegasus poem (in 'The Erl King's Shroud')